# EYE ON THE SKY

# WHEN HURRICANES HOWL

Gareth Stevens
PUBLISHING

BY BARBARA LINDE

Please visit our website, www.garethstevens.com. For a free color catalog of all our high-quality books, call toll free 1-800-542-2595 or fax 1-877-542-2596.

**Library of Congress Cataloging-in-Publication Data**

Linde, Barbara M.
When hurricanes howl / by Barbara M. Linde.
p. cm. — (Eye on the sky)
Includes index.
ISBN 978-1-4824-2888-9 (pbk.)
ISBN 978-1-4824-2889-6 (6 pack)
ISBN 978-1-4824-2890-2 (library binding)
1. Hurricanes — Juvenile literature. I. Linde, Barbara M. II. Title.
QC944.2 L56 2016
551.55'2—d23

Published in 2016 by
**Gareth Stevens Publishing**
111 East 14th Street, Suite 349
New York, NY 10003

Copyright © 2016 Gareth Stevens Publishing

Designer: Laura Bowen
Editor: Kristen Rajczak

Photo credits: Cover, pp. 1, 9 Stocktrek Images/Getty Images; cover, pp. 1–32 (series art) Nik Merkulov/Shutterstock.com; p. 5 (main) B747/Shutterstock.com; p. 5 (inset) Paul J. Richards/AFP/Getty Images; p. 7 (top) wormig/Shutterstock.com; p. 7 (bottom) Harvepino/Shutterstock.com; p. 8 Claudio Lovo/Shutterstock.com; p. 11 Vladislav Gurfinkel/Shutterstock.com; p. 13 Cathy Kovarik/Shutterstock.com; p. 15 Mechanik/Shutterstock.com; p. 16 (left) Leonard Zhukovsky/Shutterstock.com; pp. 16 (right), 27 (main) Anton Oparin/Shutterstock.com; p. 17 Mario Tama/Getty Images News/Getty Images; p. 18 (left) Jeffrey Bruno/Shutterstock.com; p. 18 (right) Glynnis Jones/Shutterstock.com; p. 19 Mishella/Shutterstock.com; p. 21 (main) NOAA/Science Source/Getty Images; p. 21 (inset) imagist/Shutterstock.com; pp. 23 (top), 25 (main) New York Public Library/Science Source/Getty Images; p. 23 (bottom) AKaiser/Shutterstock.com; p. 25 (inset) Buyenlarge/Archive Photos/Getty Images; p. 26 Lisa F. Young/Shutterstock.com; p. 27 (helicopter) Terry Poche/Shutterstock.com; p. 27 (bottles) a katz/Shutterstock.com; p. 29 (main) digidreamgrafix/Shutterstock.com; p. 29 (inset) Cvandyke/Shutterstock.com.

Printed in the United States of America

CPSIA compliance information: Batch #CS15GS: For further information contact Gareth Stevens, New York, New York at 1-800-542-2595.

# CONTENTS

Words in the glossary appear in **bold** type the first time they are used in the text.

# HURRICANE ON THE WAY

You've felt the air get thicker and wetter for the past few days. You've seen the wind change from barely moving the leaves to pushing and shoving them around. The white wisps of clouds you saw yesterday are now towering darkly above you. You keep hearing the wind shrieking and thunder rumbling. Lightning flashes every few minutes, closer with each bolt. Rain is pounding your house and forming huge puddles in the yard. The electricity is flickering, so you have your flashlight and battery-powered radio within easy reach.

What's going on? There's a hurricane howling out there!

## THE STORM GOD

The ancient Mayan people believed in a storm god named Hunraken. The Taino people in the Caribbean had a creator goddess they called Huracan. The word "hurricane" comes from the stories of these two groups, who believed their gods caused the terrible storms.

4

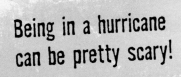

Being in a hurricane
can be pretty scary!

# WHAT IS A HURRICANE?

A tropical cyclone is a storm made of winds, clouds, and rain that forms over the warm waters near the equator.

These storms don't just pop up all at once. First, thunderstorms form, either over the ocean or near the western coast of Africa, and move toward warmer parts of the ocean. Surface water **evaporates** into the atmosphere, and the warm, moist air rises. Cool air moves in to replace the rising air, and that warms and rises, too. Higher up, the water vapor **condenses** into clouds and rain. The clouds rotate as they grow. The pattern continues as more air warms and rises.

## SAME STORM, DIFFERENT NAME

Tropical cyclones have different names in different parts of the world. The word "hurricane" refers to a tropical cyclone in the Atlantic Ocean or eastern Pacific Ocean. Storms in the western Pacific are referred to as typhoons. Storms over the Indian Ocean and southern Pacific Ocean are called cyclones.

Legend:
- areas in which tropical storms form
- typical path of storm

HURRICANES

HURRICANES

TYPHOONS

CYCLONES

CYCLONES

EQUATOR

This map shows the different names of tropical cyclones around the world as well as the direction the storms in those areas commonly move.

A hurricane is shaped like a **spiral**. North of the equator, hurricane winds rotate counterclockwise. South of the equator, the winds rotate clockwise.

At this point, a storm that has strong winds moving around a definite center is called a tropical depression. If wind pushes it toward warmer water, the tropical depression gets larger and stronger. When winds reach 39 miles (63 km) per hour, the storm is known as a tropical storm. When the swirling winds reach 74 miles (119 km) per hour, it's called a hurricane.

Most of the time, a hurricane stays in the central part of the ocean where only a few ships may feel its effects. But when it reaches land, the fierce winds and drenching rains can cause a lot of harm.

## HURRICANE SEASON

North of the equator, hurricane season officially starts on June 1 and ends on November 30. There may be hurricanes before or after those dates, but most storms fall within that time period. Most hurricanes occur during August and September, when the water is warmest.

In 2014, Hurricane Arthur was photographed from space! Its spiral shape can be seen clearly.

9

# THE PARTS OF A HURRICANE

A hurricane has several parts. The eye at the center can be as small as 5 miles (8 km) to as much as 100 miles (160 km) across! The weather in the eye is fair and calm. The most powerful wind and the heaviest rain are in the ring of clouds called the eye wall. Rain bands are wide areas of wind, rain, and thunderstorms moving out from the eye. These can stretch for hundreds of miles.

When a hurricane moves over colder water or land, it weakens, breaks apart, and finally dies. A hurricane can last anywhere from a day to several weeks.

## TORNADOES!

**Tornadoes** often form in the rain bands when a hurricane reaches land. In September 2004, Hurricane Ivan produced about 120 tornadoes or more in 9 states. This is the highest number of tornadoes ever to come from one hurricane. In general, tornadoes that form from hurricanes aren't very strong and don't last long.

**EYE**

In the eye of a hurricane, you may look up and see cloudless blue sky if it's daytime!

# THE STORMIEST STORMS

Hurricanes can be the most severe storms in the entire world! They often have a wide path and move forward for hundreds, even thousands, of miles. Uprooted **vegetation**, flying **debris**, fallen power lines, and broken glass are some of the dangers. Drowning, either on land or at sea, is also a concern.

Herb Saffir, a wind engineer, and Bob Simpson, who was the director of the National Hurricane Center, created a scale that ranks hurricanes in 1969. A hurricane is given a "category" number based on wind speed as well as the kind and amount of **damage** it causes.

## ANA, WALTER, AND THE OTHERS

Each hurricane has its own name. A committee of the World Meteorological Organization has created a list for a 6-year cycle, with names going alphabetically and alternating male and female. If a hurricane is especially destructive, its name isn't used again. If more than 21 named storms occur in a year, additional storms are named using the Greek alphabet (Alpha, Beta, Gamma, etc.).

# THE SAFFIR-SIMPSON SCALE

| CATEGORY | WIND SPEEDS | DESCRIPTION OF DAMAGE |
|---|---|---|
| 1 | 74–95 miles (119–153 km) per hour | not much damage to buildings, some tree branches break, some flooding near the coast, damage to power lines |
| 2 | 96–110 miles (154–177 km) per hour | some damage to buildings (especially mobile homes and those with weak frames), vegetation uprooted, some flooding, flying debris can cause injury, power outages |
| 3 | 111–130 miles (178–209 km) per hour | significant building damage including blown-out windows, uprooted and broken trees block roads, damage to boats and piers, inland flooding, lack of freshwater and electricity |
| 4 | 131–155 miles (210–249 km) per hour | roofs blow off buildings and homes, most trees uprooted, extensive flooding, roads blocked, evacuation of coastal areas, power outages for weeks or longer |
| 5 | greater than 155 miles (249 km) per hour | complete destruction of many buildings, much destruction of vegetation, heavy flooding, power outages for weeks or longer, area becomes generally uninhabitable for weeks or months |

Most hurricanes fall between Categories 1 and 3. There are fewer Category 4 or 5 storms. Years can go by without one.

# THE HURRICANE HUNTERS

Thanks to the members of the 53rd Weather **Reconnaissance** Squadron of the US Air Force Reserve, we know a lot about hurricanes. These "Hurricane Hunters" use an airplane with special weather **equipment**. They drop instruments into hurricanes to record wind speed, temperature, and other information. This data is sent to the National Hurricane Center. Then meteorologists make forecasts about the storm. These help people prepare for a coming storm.

The National Hurricane Center also uses satellites to track storms. What they learn helps them advise people about staying in an area or evacuating.

## HURRICANES AND CLIMATE CHANGE

Meteorologists, or the scientists who study the weather, believe that climate change is causing stronger hurricanes and higher **storm surges**. If the seas continue to get warmer, more tropical storms may become hurricanes, and those storms may have even stronger winds and rains. Scientists around the world continue to study the problem.

Satellites are objects circling Earth that are often used by scientists to gather data, including images and measurements of the weather happening on Earth.

15

# SUPERSTORM SANDY

Hurricane Sandy formed around October 23, 2012, very late in hurricane season. After causing 51 deaths and great damage in Jamaica, Haiti, and Cuba, Sandy moved into the Atlantic Ocean. It made landfall near Atlantic City, New Jersey, on October 29.

Several weather events combined to give Sandy the nicknames "Superstorm" and "Frankenstorm." It hit the coast at high tide on the night of a full moon. Sandy also bumped into winter-like weather from the north and west, which made the storm larger and stronger. Its winds stretched for 900 miles (1,448 km)! Heavy snow hit areas around the Appalachian Mountains.

# MANTOLOKING

In 2005, the newest Mantoloking Bridge opened to connect the **barrier island** town of Mantoloking to mainland New Jersey. When Sandy hit, the bridge was completely underwater. Sand and debris made it impassable. Houses were completely washed away by the storm surge. A new inlet was created, connecting the Atlantic Ocean to the Jones Tide Pond on the island's other side.

This photo shows the barrier island town of Mantoloking, New Jersey, after Hurricane Sandy made landfall there.

Sandy's combination of wind and high tide caused storm surges along the coast from Florida to Maine! The worst storm surge was in New Jersey. Buildings, coastal amusement park rides, and cars were damaged by the wind and dragged out to sea. The sizes and shapes of beaches were changed. Storm surges of up to 14 feet (4.3 m) caused floods in New York City, including parts of its subway system.

Some people lost everything. Schools and businesses were closed for days. Rescue workers had trouble getting to those who were trapped because the streets were either flooded or ripped apart. Recovery took years.

## FRANKENSTORM FACTS

- Over 8 million homes in 17 states lost electric power.
- Over 11 million people had no transportation when trains and buses stopped running and the airports shut down.
- The cost of the storm was more than $50 billion.
- The World Meteorological Organization retired the name "Sandy" from the list of Atlantic hurricane names.

The flooding from Hurricane Sandy caused car crashes and many other problems.

# DEVASTATING KATRINA

Katrina was one of the worst hurricanes to ever affect the United States. It first made landfall near Miami, Florida, on August 25, 2005, as a Category 1 storm, dropping about 14 inches (35.6 cm) of rain. By the time it reached Buras, Louisiana, Katrina was a Category 3 storm with a width of over 415 miles (668 km). The storm surge along the Gulf Coast of Mississippi was almost 28 feet (8.5 m), the highest ever recorded.

Katrina caused about $125 billion in damage, totally destroyed thousands of buildings, and wiped highways right off the map. It killed over 1,800 people.

## THE NEW ORLEANS LEVEES

Katrina's storm surge in New Orleans, Louisiana, was one of the worst in history. The city, which sits mostly below sea level, was surrounded by levees. A levee is a mound of earth and other matter used to prevent flooding. However, many of the city's levees broke from the huge amounts of water, flooding much of the city and its surrounding area for miles inland. Thousands of people became homeless. Many left the city, never to return.

Entire neighborhoods in New Orleans were destroyed when the levees broke.

# CATASTROPHIC CAMILLE

Hurricane Camille reached Category 5 strength on August 16, 1969, and hit Bay Saint Louis, Mississippi, around 9 p.m. on August 17. The winds reached about 200 miles (322 km) per hour, flattening buildings along the Mississippi coast. Since all the storm-measuring equipment was destroyed, scientists think the winds may have been even stronger. Storm surges of about 24 feet (7.3 m) flooded streets up to four blocks from the coast. The rain and waves split several barrier islands in two!

Weakening upon landfall, Camille drenched Virginia and West Virginia with more than 20 inches (51 cm) of rain in about 5 hours. Huge walls of mud slid down mountainsides, uprooting forests and burying homes.

## THE BACKWARD MISSISSIPPI RIVER

Strong waves and wind pushed water from the mouth of the Mississippi River back up into its channel. The river flowed backward for about 125 miles (200 km) from Venice, Louisiana, to New Orleans. This backward flow happened again during Hurricane Katrina in 2005 and Hurricane Isaac in 2012.

Hurricane Camille caused over $1.4 billion in damage and killed more than 250 people.

tropical depression
tropical storm
hurricane
major hurricane

CAMILLE 1969

**23**

# MORE HORRIFIC HURRICANES

- **1749: Hurricane of October** Meteorologists think this was a Category 4 storm and maybe one of the strongest Mid-Atlantic region storms ever.

- **1821: Cape May Hurricane** This Category 4 hurricane made landfall at Cape May, New Jersey, on September 3. Wind gusts reached 200 miles (322 km) per hour. William Redfield, an amateur meteorologist, took notes during the storm. His research helped others study hurricanes.

- **1900: Galveston Hurricane** On September 8, 1900, this Category 4 storm flooded Galveston, Texas. Between 6,000 and 8,000 people died in Galveston. Thousands of other deaths in the area occurred because of the storm, too.

## THE TEMPEST BY WILLIAM SHAKESPEARE

In 1609, a fleet of ships was sailing from England to the new colony at Jamestown, Virginia. Most of the ships were lost in a terrible storm, but the *Sea Venture* was blown off course and landed in Bermuda. The passengers and crew were stranded there for months. Many people think that William Shakespeare based his play *The Tempest* on this event.

The Galveston Hurricane is still the deadliest hurricane ever in the United States.

# SURVIVING A HURRICANE

All during hurricane season, weather forecasters let people know about storms. They declare a hurricane watch when a hurricane might be building. A hurricane warning means a storm is on its way. A warning is usually given about 36 hours before a hurricane is supposed to reach an area. This gives people time to either prepare or evacuate.

Once a hurricane hits, the safest place to be is the inside part of a building, away from windows and doors. An upper floor is better if there's flooding, but a lower floor is better if there isn't flooding.

Boarding up windows keeps people inside a home safer.

Members of the military help in the aftermath of a hurricane.

## TO THE RESCUE!

The Federal Emergency Management Agency (FEMA) helps states during **disasters**. It might bring in aid workers or provide temporary shelters or food. It gives money to states to help rebuild. The different branches of the military may send people to rescue stranded victims or to repair damaged areas. Churches and other groups often help, too.

27

# BENEFITS FROM HURRICANES

It might seem hard to believe, but there are some benefits from hurricanes. For barrier islands, wind and waves often push more sand onto their shores, making them larger and taller. Many areas need the rains that hurricanes bring. The wave action brings **nutrients** from the deeper parts of the ocean to the surface, providing more food for ocean creatures.

Along the Outer Banks of North Carolina in 1846, a hurricane pushed water from Pamlico Sound across a narrow barrier island into the Atlantic Ocean. The barrier island was cut in two, creating Oregon Inlet. Since then, people have used the inlet for recreation and transportation.

## WHAT'S NEXT?

Whether it's called Ike, Chantal, or Omar, a hurricane is part of nature, and there will always be another one. The best we can do is stay ready! Many people keep a special battery–powered radio that gives information from the National Weather Service all the time. Have a first aid and safety kit, flashlights, and food that won't spoil ready if a hurricane hits!

28

Oregon Inlet runs between the Pamlico Sound and the Atlantic Ocean, and separates Pea and Bodie Islands.

POPS

# GLOSSARY

**barrier island:** a landform made of sand that is parallel to the coast

**condense:** to change from a gas into a liquid

**damage:** harm. Also, to cause harm.

**debris:** the remains of something that has been broken

**disaster:** an event that causes much suffering or loss

**equipment:** tools, clothing, and other items needed for a job

**evacuation:** the withdrawal from a place for protection

**evaporate:** to change from a liquid to a gas

**nutrient:** something a living thing needs to grow and stay alive

**reconnaissance:** the exploration of a place to collect information

**spiral:** a shape with a center point and a line curling around the point, further away each time

**storm surge:** the rise of water above the usual tide, caused by a storm

**tornado:** a storm featuring swirling winds and a funnel-shaped cloud

**vegetation:** trees, bushes, and other plants

# FOR MORE INFORMATION

## BOOKS

Gray-Wilburn, Renee. *Hurricanes: Be Aware and Prepare.* North Mankato, MN: Capstone Press, 2015.

Treaster, Joseph B. *Hurricane Force: In the Path of America's Deadliest Storms.* Boston, MA: Kingfisher, 2007.

## WEBSITES

**Hurricane Names—How Are Hurricanes Named?**
*geology.com/hurricanes/hurricane-names.shtml*
Is your name on the list of hurricanes for a particular year?
Find out here!

**Hurricanes**
*www.weatherwizkids.com/weather-hurricane.htm*
Learn how hurricanes form and find out some safety tips.
Download a hurricane-tracking chart.

**Hurricanes 101**
*video.nationalgeographic.com/video/101-videos/hurricanes-101*
Have a safe, virtual encounter with a hurricane as you watch these videos.

# INDEX